*For anyone who's ever had five minutes
to accomplish thirty things
that all needed to be completed two hours ago.*

HEALTHY IN A HURRY

Your Guide to Quick and Easy Weeknight Meals

TABLE OF CONTENTS

SALAD

Caprese Pasta Salad | **37**
Chicken Caesar Salad | **38**
Greek Couscous Salad | **39**
Quinoa Salad with Grilled Chicken | **40**
Tuna Nicoise Salad | **41**

SOUP/STEW

Egg Drop Soup | **42**
Lentil and Tomato Soup | **43**
Ramen Noodle Soup | **44**
Roasted Red Pepper Soup | **45**
Sausage and White Bean Stew | **46**
Taco Soup | **47**
Turkey and Bean Chili | **48**

VEGETARIAN

Chickpea and Spinach Curry | **49**
Egg Salad Sandwiches | **50**
Eggplant Parmesan | **51**
Enchiladas | **52**
Falafel Wraps with Tzatziki | **53**
Hummus and Veggie Wraps | **54**
Loaded Vegetable Quesadillas | **55**
Margherita Pizza | **56**
Quiche Lorraine | **57**
Quinoa Fried "Rice" | **58**
Quinoa Stuffed Peppers | **59**
Rainbow Vegetable Stir-Fry | **60**
Ratatouille with Polenta | **61**
Risotto Primavera | **62**
Soba Noodles with Ginger Sesame Dressing | **63**
Spinach and Feta Frittata | **64**
Sweet Potato and Black Bean Tacos | **65**

ASIAN BEEF STIR-FRY

PREP THE STIR-FRY SAUCE: In a small bowl, whisk together the soy sauce, rice vinegar, and cornstarch until well combined. Set aside.

COOK THE BEEF: Heat the olive oil in a large wok or skillet over medium-high heat. Add the beef slices and cook until browned, about 2-3 minutes. Season with salt and pepper, then remove the beef from the skillet and set aside.

COOK THE VEGETABLES: In the same skillet, add the broccoli, red bell pepper, snap peas, and carrots. Cook for about 4-5 minutes, or until the vegetables are just tender.

ADD THE AROMATICS: Add the minced garlic and ginger to the skillet and cook until fragrant, about 1 minute.

COMBINE: Return the beef to the skillet and pour over the prepared stir-fry sauce. Toss everything together and cook for another 2-3 minutes, until the sauce has thickened.

SERVE: Divide the stir-fry among four plates. Garnish with sesame seeds and sliced green onions.

INGREDIENTS:

1 lb beef sirloin, thinly sliced
1 tablespoon olive oil
2 cups broccoli florets
1 red bell pepper, thinly sliced
1 cup snap peas
2 carrots, sliced into thin rounds
2 cloves garlic, minced
1 tablespoon fresh ginger, minced
3 tablespoons low-sodium soy sauce
2 tablespoons rice vinegar
1 tablespoon cornstarch
Salt and pepper to taste
Toasted sesame seeds and sliced green onions, for garnish

SERVES 4

This recipe also works great with chicken, seafood, and pork!

AUTHOR'S NOTE

BEEF AND BROCCOLI

INGREDIENTS:

1 lb lean beef (such as flank steak), thinly sliced
Salt and pepper to taste
2 tablespoons olive oil, divided
4 cups broccoli florets
3 cloves garlic, minced
1/4 cup low-sodium soy sauce
2 tablespoons cornstarch
1 cup beef broth
1 tablespoon honey
2 teaspoons sesame oil
Toasted sesame seeds, for garnish (optional)

SERVES 4

PREPARE THE BEEF: Season the beef slices with salt and pepper.

SAUTÉ THE BEEF: Heat 1 tablespoon of the olive oil in a large skillet or wok over medium-high heat. Add the beef and stir-fry until it is mostly browned, about 2-3 minutes. Transfer the beef to a plate and set it aside.

COOK THE BROCCOLI: In the same skillet, add the remaining 1 tablespoon of olive oil. Add the broccoli florets and stir-fry until they are bright green and tender-crisp, about 3-4 minutes.

MAKE THE SAUCE: In a small bowl, whisk together the garlic, soy sauce, cornstarch, beef broth, honey, and sesame oil. Pour this mixture into the skillet with the broccoli.

COMBINE AND SIMMER: Return the beef to the skillet. Stir everything together to coat in the sauce. Simmer for about 2-3 minutes, or until the sauce has thickened.

SERVE: Divide the Beef and Broccoli between four plates. Sprinkle with sesame seeds if desired, and serve immediately.

EMPANADAS

INGREDIENTS:

1 tablespoon olive oil
1 pound lean ground beef
1 onion, diced
1 bell pepper, diced
2 cloves of garlic, minced
1 teaspoon cumin
Salt and pepper to taste
1 cup low-fat cheese (like cheddar or
Monterey Jack), shredded
1 package (8 count) whole wheat empanada
dough (found in the frozen food aisle)
1 egg, beaten for egg wash

SERVES 4

Get creative with the filling and try different protein and vegetable combos!

AUTHOR'S NOTE

PREHEAT THE OVEN: Preheat your oven to 375°F and line a baking sheet with parchment paper.

COOK THE FILLING: In a large skillet, heat the olive oil over medium heat. Add the ground beef, onion, bell pepper, and garlic, and cook until the beef is browned and the vegetables are tender. Season with cumin, salt, and pepper.

ASSEMBLE THE EMPANADAS: Spoon a portion of the beef mixture onto one half of each empanada round, leaving a border around the edge. Sprinkle a bit of cheese on top of the filling. Fold the dough over the filling to create a half-moon shape and crimp the edges with a fork to seal.

BAKE THE EMPANADAS: Place the empanadas on the prepared baking sheet and brush the tops with the beaten egg. Bake for 20-25 minutes, or until golden brown.

SERVE: Allow the empanadas to cool slightly before serving. Enjoy with a side of salsa, guacamole, or a fresh salad!

PAN-SEARED STEAK

INGREDIENTS:

4 steaks (such as sirloin, ribeye, or filet mignon; about 6 ounces each)
Salt and pepper to taste
1 tablespoon olive oil
2 cloves garlic, peeled and smashed
2 sprigs fresh rosemary or thyme
2 tablespoons unsalted butter

SERVES 4

PREPARE THE STEAK: Allow the steaks to sit at room temperature for about 15 minutes. Season both sides of each steak generously with salt and pepper.

SEAR THE STEAK: Heat the olive oil in a large heavy skillet (preferably cast iron) over medium-high heat. When the oil is hot but not smoking, add the steaks. Cook without moving for about 3-4 minutes, or until a crust forms. Flip the steaks and cook for another 3-4 minutes for medium-rare, or longer to your desired level of doneness.

ADD AROMATICS: Reduce the heat to medium. Add the smashed garlic and rosemary or thyme sprigs to the skillet. Tilt the skillet towards you so that the oil and juices collect at the bottom.

BASTE THE STEAK: Add the butter to the skillet. When it's melted, use a spoon to baste the steaks with the flavored butter for about 1-2 minutes.

REST THE STEAK: Remove the skillet from the heat. Transfer the steaks to a cutting board and let them rest for at least 5 minutes to allow the juices to redistribute.

SERVE: Slice the steak against the grain if desired, and serve immediately.

CHICKEN FAJITAS

INGREDIENTS:

1 lb chicken breasts, sliced into thin strips
3 bell peppers (a mix of colors), thinly sliced
1 large onion, thinly sliced
2 tablespoons olive oil
1 tablespoon chili powder
1 teaspoon ground cumin
Salt and pepper to taste
8 whole-grain tortillas
1/2 cup salsa
Optional toppings: sliced avocado, fresh cilantro, lime wedges, sour cream, or shredded cheese

SERVES 4

This recipe also works great with beef, seafood, tofu or mixed roasted vegetables!

AUTHOR'S NOTE

SEASON THE CHICKEN: Toss the chicken strips with chili powder, cumin, salt, and pepper in a large bowl.

COOK THE CHICKEN: Heat 1 tablespoon of the olive oil in a large skillet over medium-high heat. Add the chicken and cook until it's no longer pink in the middle, about 5-7 minutes. Remove the chicken from the skillet and set it aside.

COOK THE VEGETABLES: Add the remaining 1 tablespoon of olive oil to the skillet. Add the bell peppers and onion, and cook until they're tender and slightly charred, about 5-7 minutes.

COMBINE: Return the chicken to the skillet and stir everything together. Cook for another 2 minutes, or until everything is heated through.

PREPARE THE FAJITAS: Warm the tortillas according to the package instructions. Spoon the chicken and vegetable mixture onto each tortilla. Top with salsa and any other toppings you like.

SERVE: Fold the tortillas over the filling, and serve immediately.

CHICKEN PARMESAN

INGREDIENTS:

4 boneless, skinless chicken breasts (about 1 pound)
Salt and pepper to taste
1 tablespoon olive oil
1/2 cup Parmesan cheese, grated
1 cup marinara sauce, store-bought or homemade
1 cup mozzarella cheese, shredded
2 tablespoons chopped fresh basil, for garnish

SERVES 4

This recipe can be served with a salad or over whole wheat penne, lentil or chickpea pasta.

PREPARE THE CHICKEN: Season the chicken breasts on both sides with salt and pepper.

SAUTÉ THE CHICKEN: Heat the olive oil in a large, oven-safe skillet over medium heat. Add the chicken and cook until golden and cooked through, about 5 minutes per side. Remove the chicken from the skillet and set aside.

PREPARE THE SAUCE: Pour the marinara sauce into the skillet, scraping up any browned bits from the bottom with a wooden spoon. Bring the sauce to a simmer.

ASSEMBLE THE CHICKEN PARMESAN: Return the chicken to the skillet, nestling it into the sauce. Spoon a little sauce over each breast, then sprinkle evenly with the Parmesan cheese, followed by the mozzarella cheese.

BROIL THE CHICKEN PARMESAN: Place the skillet under your oven's broiler and broil until the cheese is melted and bubbly, about 2-3 minutes. Keep a close eye on it to prevent burning.

SERVE: Sprinkle the Chicken Parmesan with fresh basil and serve immediately, spooning extra sauce from the skillet onto each plate.

AUTHOR'S NOTE

CHICKEN LETTUCE WRAPS

COOK THE CHICKEN: Heat the sesame oil in a large skillet over medium heat. Add the ground chicken, season with salt and pepper, and cook until browned and cooked through, about 5-7 minutes. Make sure to break up the chicken into small crumbles while it cooks.

SAUTÉ THE AROMATICS: Add the minced garlic, grated ginger, diced bell pepper, and chopped green onions to the skillet. Stir and cook until the vegetables are tender, about 3-5 minutes.

ADD THE SAUCES: Stir in the hoisin sauce and soy sauce, coating the chicken and vegetables evenly. Cook for another 2 minutes to let the flavors meld together.

PREPARE THE LETTUCE WRAPS: Spoon a generous amount of the hoisin chicken mixture into each lettuce leaf.

SERVE: Garnish the lettuce wraps with sesame seeds, shredded carrot, and chopped green onion and serve immediately.

INGREDIENTS:

1 tablespoon sesame oil
1 pound ground chicken
Salt and pepper to taste
2 cloves garlic, minced
1 tablespoon fresh ginger, grated
1 bell pepper, diced
3 green onions, chopped
1/4 cup hoisin sauce
1 tablespoon soy sauce
1 head Bibb or iceberg lettuce, leaves separated
Sesame seeds, shredded carrot, and chopped green onion, for garnish

SERVES 4

KUNG PAO CHICKEN

PREPARE THE CHICKEN: Season the chicken pieces with salt and pepper.

COOK THE CHICKEN: Heat the vegetable oil in a large pan or wok over medium-high heat. Add the chicken and cook until browned and cooked through, about 5-7 minutes. Remove the chicken from the pan and set aside.

COOK THE VEGETABLES: In the same pan, add the diced red bell pepper and zucchini. Cook until the vegetables are tender, about 5 minutes.

SAUTÉ THE AROMATICS: Add the minced garlic and grated ginger to the pan, and sauté for an additional minute.

MAKE THE SAUCE: In a small bowl, whisk together the soy sauce, rice vinegar, hoisin sauce, and cornstarch until smooth. Pour the sauce into the pan with the vegetables and cook until the sauce has thickened, about 2 minutes.

COMBINE AND ADD THE PEANUTS: Return the cooked chicken to the pan and toss to coat in the sauce. Stir in the peanuts.

SERVE: Top the dish with the sliced green onions just before serving. Serve over cooked rice if desired.

INGREDIENTS:

2 boneless, skinless chicken breasts, cut into bite-sized pieces
Salt and pepper to taste
1 tablespoon vegetable oil
1 red bell pepper, diced
1 zucchini, diced
4 cloves garlic, minced
1 teaspoon fresh ginger, grated
1/4 cup low-sodium soy sauce
1 tablespoon rice vinegar
2 teaspoons hoisin sauce
2 teaspoons cornstarch
1/2 cup unsalted dry roasted peanuts
2 green onions, sliced
Cooked rice for serving (optional)

SERVES 4

SPINACH AND FETA STUFFED CHICKEN

INGREDIENTS:

4 boneless, skinless chicken breasts
Salt and pepper to taste
2 tablespoons olive oil
2 cups fresh spinach, chopped
2 cloves garlic, minced
1/2 cup feta cheese, crumbled
1 teaspoon dried oregano
Toothpicks for securing the chicken

SERVES 4

PREPARE THE CHICKEN: Preheat your oven to 375°F. Season the chicken breasts with salt and pepper. Cut a horizontal slit in each chicken breast to create a pocket, but be careful not to cut all the way through.

COOK THE SPINACH: Heat 1 tablespoon of the olive oil in a skillet over medium heat. Add the spinach and garlic, and cook until the spinach is wilted, about 2-3 minutes.

MAKE THE STUFFING: Remove the skillet from the heat. Stir in the feta cheese and oregano until well combined.

STUFF THE CHICKEN: Spoon the spinach and feta mixture into the pockets of the chicken breasts. Secure the openings with toothpicks.

COOK THE CHICKEN: Heat the remaining 1 tablespoon of olive oil in the skillet over medium-high heat. Add the chicken breasts and sear them on each side until golden brown, about 3-4 minutes per side.

BAKE: Transfer the skillet to the oven, and bake for 10-12 minutes, or until the chicken is cooked through and no longer pink in the middle.

SERVE: Carefully remove the toothpicks, and serve!

THAI BASIL CHICKEN

COOK THE CHICKEN: Heat the canola oil in a large skillet or wok over medium-high heat. Add the chicken and season with salt and pepper. Cook until the chicken is cooked through and browned, about 5-7 minutes. Remove the chicken from the skillet and set it aside.

SAUTÉ THE VEGETABLES: In the same skillet, add the garlic, bell pepper, and onion. Sauté until the vegetables are tender, about 5 minutes.

COMBINE THE REMAINING INGREDIENTS: Return the chicken to the skillet. Add the soy sauce, oyster sauce, and sugar. Stir to combine and heat until everything is well coated and heated through, about 2 minutes.

ADD THE BASIL: Stir in the Thai basil leaves and cook for an additional minute, or until the basil is wilted. Add the sliced chili peppers if using.

SERVE: Serve hot, with steamed rice or quinoa if desired.

INGREDIENTS:

1 1/2 pounds boneless, skinless chicken breasts or thighs, thinly sliced
1 tablespoon canola oil
2 cloves garlic, minced
1 red bell pepper, sliced thin
1 medium onion, sliced thin
3 tablespoons low-sodium soy sauce or fish sauce
1 tablespoon oyster sauce
1 teaspoon sugar
1/2 cup fresh Thai basil leaves
1-2 bird's eye chili peppers, sliced (optional, for heat)
Salt and pepper to taste

SERVES 4

FISH TACOS

PREPARE THE SLAW: In a large bowl, combine the shredded cabbage, Greek yogurt, lime juice, and chili powder. Season with salt and pepper, and stir well. Set aside.

COOK THE FISH: Season the fish fillets with salt and pepper. Heat the olive oil in a large non-stick skillet over medium-high heat. Add the fish and cook for 2-3 minutes per side, or until cooked through and flaky. Remove from heat.

ASSEMBLE THE TACOS: Warm the corn tortillas in a dry skillet or directly over a gas flame until pliable. Divide the cooked fish between the tortillas. Top with the prepared slaw, shredded lettuce, and sliced avocado.

SERVE: Garnish with fresh cilantro and serve with lime wedges on the side for squeezing.

INGREDIENTS:

1 lb white fish fillets (like cod or tilapia)
Salt and pepper to taste
1 tablespoon olive oil
8 small corn tortillas
2 cups lettuce, shredded
1 ripe avocado, sliced
Fresh cilantro and lime wedges, for garnish

FOR THE SLAW:
2 cups cabbage (or coleslaw mix), shredded
1/2 cup Greek yogurt
1 tablespoon lime juice
1/2 teaspoon chili powder
Salt and pepper to taste

SERVES 4

HONEY-SOY GLAZED SALMON

PREPARE THE SALMON: Season the salmon fillets on both sides with salt and pepper.

MAKE THE SAUCE: In a small bowl, whisk together the honey, soy sauce, garlic, and ginger.

SEAR THE SALMON: Heat the olive oil in a large non-stick skillet over medium-high heat. Add the salmon, skin side up, and cook until browned, about 4 minutes.

ADD THE SAUCE: Flip the salmon and pour the honey-soy mixture over the fillets. Reduce the heat to medium, cover the skillet, and let the salmon cook for another 4-6 minutes, or until the fillets are cooked through and the glaze has thickened.

FINISH AND SERVE: Garnish the salmon with chopped green onions and sesame seeds before serving.

INGREDIENTS:

4 salmon fillets (around 6 ounces each)
Salt and pepper to taste
3 tablespoons honey
2 tablespoons low sodium soy sauce
2 cloves garlic, minced
1 tablespoon fresh ginger, grated
1 tablespoon olive oil
Chopped green onions and sesame seeds, for garnish

SERVES 4

LEMON HERB SALMON WITH QUINOA SALAD

INGREDIENTS:

4 salmon fillets (4-6 ounces each)
2 tablespoons olive oil
Zest and juice of 1 lemon
2 cloves garlic, minced
2 tablespoons fresh dill, chopped
Salt and pepper to taste

FOR THE SALAD:
1 cup quinoa
2 cups water or chicken broth
1 cucumber, diced
1 red bell pepper, diced
1/2 cup cherry tomatoes, halved
1/4 cup fresh parsley, chopped
1/4 cup fresh mint, chopped
2 tablespoons olive oil
Juice of 1 lemon
Salt and pepper to taste

SERVES 4

PREPARE THE SALMON: Preheat the oven to 400°F. Place the salmon fillets on a baking sheet lined with parchment paper. Mix together the olive oil, lemon zest, lemon juice, minced garlic, dill, salt, and pepper in a small bowl. Spoon this mixture evenly over the salmon fillets.

BAKE THE SALMON: Bake the salmon in the preheated oven for 12-15 minutes, or until it flakes easily with a fork.

PREPARE THE QUINOA SALAD: While the salmon is baking, rinse the quinoa under cold water until the water runs clear. In a medium-sized saucepan, bring the 2 cups of water or chicken broth to a boil. Add the rinsed quinoa, reduce heat to low, cover the pot, and let it simmer for about 15 minutes, or until all the liquid is absorbed.

FLUFF AND COOL: Once cooked, remove the quinoa from heat and fluff it with a fork. Allow it to cool slightly.

PREPARE THE SALAD: In a large bowl, combine the cooled quinoa, diced cucumber, diced red bell pepper, halved cherry tomatoes, chopped parsley, and chopped mint.

DRESS THE SALAD: In a small bowl, whisk together the olive oil, lemon juice, salt, and pepper to make the dressing. Pour this dressing over the quinoa salad and mix well.

SERVE: Serve the baked salmon fillets with a side of the quinoa salad.

SALMON POKE BOWLS

MARINATE THE SALMON: In a medium bowl, mix together the diced salmon, soy sauce, sesame oil, rice vinegar, and honey. Cover and let marinate in the refrigerator for at least 15 minutes.

PREPARE THE BOWLS: Divide the cooked quinoa evenly among four bowls.

PLATE AND GARNISH: Top each bowl with an equal amount of the marinated salmon, diced avocado, cucumber, shredded carrot, sliced green onions, sesame seeds, and edamame beans.

FINISH AND SERVE: Drizzle some of the marinade over the top of each bowl for extra flavor. Serve immediately and enjoy!

INGREDIENTS:

1 pound of sushi-grade salmon, diced
1/4 cup of low-sodium soy sauce
1 tablespoon of sesame oil
1 teaspoon of rice vinegar
1 teaspoon of honey
1 cup of cooked quinoa
1 avocado, sliced
1 cucumber, sliced
1 carrot, shredded
2 green onions, sliced
1 tablespoon of sesame seeds
1/2 cup of edamame beans, shelled
Salt to taste

SERVES 4

SHRIMP PO' BOY

INGREDIENTS:

1 pound medium shrimp, peeled and deveined
Salt and pepper to taste
1/2 cup whole wheat flour
1 egg, beaten
1 cup panko bread crumbs
1/4 cup mayonnaise
1 tablespoon Dijon mustard
1 tablespoon sweet pickle relish
4 whole wheat baguettes, split lengthwise
2 cups lettuce, shredded
1 large tomato, sliced
1/4 cup pickles, sliced

SERVES 4

PREHEAT THE OVEN: Preheat your oven to 425°F and line a baking sheet with parchment paper.

SEASON THE SHRIMP: Season the shrimp with salt and pepper, then dredge in flour, dip in egg, and coat in panko breadcrumbs. Arrange the shrimp on the prepared baking sheet in a single layer.

BAKE THE SHRIMP: Bake the shrimp in the preheated oven for 10-12 minutes, or until golden brown and cooked through.

MAKE THE SUACE: While the shrimp is baking, in a small bowl, combine the mayonnaise, Dijon mustard, and sweet pickle relish to make the remoulade sauce. Set aside.

ASSEMBLE AND SERVE: To assemble the sandwiches, spread a generous amount of the remoulade sauce on both halves of each baguette. Layer the lettuce, tomato slices, pickles, and baked shrimp on the bottom halves of the baguettes. Top with the other half of the baguettes to complete the sandwiches.

SHRIMP AND CHORIZO PAELLA

INGREDIENTS:

2 tablespoons olive oil
1/2 pound raw shrimp, peeled and deveined
1/2 pound chorizo sausage, sliced into rounds
1 small onion, diced
3 cloves garlic, minced
1 red bell pepper, diced
1 1/2 cups short-grain rice, rinsed
3 cups low-sodium chicken broth
1 cup canned tomatoes, diced
1/2 teaspoon smoked paprika
1/2 teaspoon saffron threads
1 cup frozen peas
Salt and pepper to taste
Lemon wedges and chopped fresh parsley, for serving

SERVES 4

COOK THE SHRIMP: Heat 1 tablespoon of olive oil in a large skillet over medium-high heat. Add the shrimp and cook until pink and opaque, about 2-3 minutes per side. Remove the shrimp from the skillet and set aside.

COOK THE CHORIZO: In the same skillet, add the remaining 1 tablespoon of olive oil and the chorizo. Cook until the chorizo is browned, about 5 minutes.

ADD THE VEGETABLES: Add the onion, garlic, and bell pepper to the skillet. Cook until the vegetables are softened, about 5 minutes.

COMBINE THE REMAINING INGREDIENTS: Stir in the rice, chicken broth, diced tomatoes, smoked paprika, and saffron. Season with salt and pepper. Bring the mixture to a boil, then reduce the heat to low, cover, and simmer until the rice is cooked and has absorbed most of the liquid, about 15 minutes.

ADD THE PEAS AND SHRIMP: Stir in the frozen peas and cooked shrimp. Cook for an additional 2-3 minutes, until everything is heated through.

FINISH AND SERVE: Serve the paella hot, garnished with lemon wedges and chopped fresh parsley.

SHRIMP PAD THAI

INGREDIENTS:

8 ounces flat rice noodles
1 pound large shrimp, peeled and deveined
Salt and pepper to taste
2 tablespoons olive oil
2 cloves garlic, minced
2 eggs, lightly beaten
1 cup bean sprouts
1 red bell pepper, thinly sliced
3 green onions, chopped
1/4 cup unsalted peanuts, chopped
1 lime, cut into wedges
Chopped fresh cilantro, for garnish

FOR THE SAUCE:
3 tablespoons fish sauce
1 tablespoon tamarind paste
1 tablespoon sugar

SERVES 4

PREPARE THE NOODLES: Cook the rice noodles according to package instructions, then drain and set aside.

SEASON THE SHRIMP: Season the shrimp with salt and pepper to taste.

PREPARE THE SAUCE: In a small bowl, combine the fish sauce, tamarind paste, and sugar. Stir until the sugar has dissolved and set aside.

COOK THE SHRIMP: Heat the olive oil in a large pan or wok over medium-high heat. Add the shrimp and cook until they turn pink, about 2-3 minutes per side. Remove the shrimp from the pan and set aside.

COOK THE EGGS: In the same pan, add the beaten eggs. Stir briefly to scramble, then let cook undisturbed until set, about 2 minutes. Remove the eggs from the pan and set aside with the shrimp.

SAUTÉ THE VEGETABLES: Add the minced garlic, bean sprouts, sliced bell pepper, and chopped green onions to the pan. Stir-fry over high heat until the vegetables are just tender, about 2 minutes.

COMBINE: Add the cooked noodles, shrimp, eggs, and prepared sauce to the pan. Toss well to combine and heat through.

SERVE: Divide the Pad Thai among four plates. Garnish with chopped peanuts, a lime wedge, and fresh cilantro before serving.

This dish can easily be adjusted to suit you or your guests taste by using chicken or vegetables in place of shrimp.

AUTHOR'S NOTE

SHRIMP SCAMPI WITH ZUCCHINI NOODLES

INGREDIENTS:

1 lb large shrimp, peeled and deveined
4 medium zucchini
2 tablespoons olive oil
4 cloves garlic, minced
1/2 cup white wine (or low-sodium chicken broth)
Juice and zest of 1 lemon
1/2 teaspoon crushed red pepper flakes (optional)
Salt and pepper to taste
2 tablespoons chopped fresh parsley
Grated Parmesan cheese, for serving (optional)

SERVES 4

PREPARE THE ZUCCHINI NOODLES: Using a spiralizer, turn the zucchini into noodles. If you don't have a spiralizer, you can use a peeler to create thin ribbons. Set aside.

COOK THE SHRIMP: Heat the olive oil in a large skillet over medium heat. Add the shrimp to the skillet and cook until pink, about 2 minutes on each side. Remove the shrimp from the skillet and set aside.

PREPARE THE SAUCE: In the same skillet, add the minced garlic and cook until fragrant, about 1 minute. Add the white wine (or chicken broth), lemon juice, lemon zest, crushed red pepper flakes (if using), salt, and pepper. Bring to a simmer and let cook for 2-3 minutes.

COMBINE: Return the shrimp to the skillet and add the zucchini noodles. Toss everything together and cook for an additional 2-3 minutes, just until the zucchini noodles are tender.

SERVE: Divide the shrimp and zucchini noodles between four plates. Sprinkle with fresh parsley and grated Parmesan cheese, if desired.

SHRIMP TACOS WITH MANGO SALSA

INGREDIENTS:

FOR THE SHRIMP:
1 pound large shrimp, peeled and deveined
1 tablespoon olive oil
1 teaspoon chili powder
Zest and juice of 1 lime
Salt to taste

FOR THE MANGO SALSA:
1 ripe mango, peeled and diced
1 small red onion, finely chopped
1 jalapeño, seeded and finely chopped
1/4 cup fresh cilantro, chopped
Juice of 1 lime
Salt to taste

FOR THE TACOS:
8 small corn or flour tortillas
1 cup shredded lettuce
1 avocado, sliced

SERVES 4

PREPARE THE SHRIMP: In a bowl, combine the shrimp, olive oil, chili powder, lime zest, lime juice, and salt. Toss until the shrimp are evenly coated. Set aside to marinate for about 10 minutes.

PREPARE THE MANGO SALSA: In another bowl, combine the diced mango, chopped red onion, jalapeño, cilantro, lime juice, and salt. Stir until well combined. Set aside.

COOK THE SHRIMP: Heat a large non-stick skillet over medium-high heat. Add the shrimp in a single layer and cook until they turn pink, about 2 minutes per side.

WARM THE TORTILLAS: While the shrimp are cooking, warm the tortillas in a dry skillet over medium heat or directly over the flame of a gas stove.

ASSEMBLE THE TACOS: On each warmed tortilla, place a handful of shredded lettuce, a few slices of avocado, and a serving of cooked shrimp. Top with a generous spoonful of mango salsa.

SERVE: Serve the tacos immediately, with extra mango salsa on the side if desired.

CHICKEN ALFREDO

PREPARE THE CHICKEN: Season chicken breasts with salt and pepper. Heat olive oil in a large skillet over medium heat. Add the chicken breasts and cook for about 5-7 minutes on each side, or until cooked through. Remove from the pan and let rest.

COOK THE PASTA: While the chicken is cooking, bring a large pot of salted water to a boil. Add the whole wheat fettuccine and cook according to package instructions until al dente. Drain, reserving 1 cup of the pasta water.

MAKE THE SAUCE: In a medium bowl, whisk together egg yolk and heavy cream until combined; set aside. Over medium-high heat, melt butter in same skillet as the chicken. Add the garlic and sauté until fragrant. Pour the cream and yolk mixture into the garlic butter and stir to combine. Reduce heat to medium-low and heat until hot, not boiling, then reduce to low.

CUT THE CHICKEN: Once the chicken breast has cooled, cut into one to two inch chunks.

COMBINE: Add the chicken and cooked pasta to the sauce with a little pasta water, as needed to thin, and toss to coat in sauce. Add the Parmesan cheese and continue to toss until well combined. The sauce should be decadent and thick. Season with salt and pepper to taste, if needed.

SERVE: Divide the Alfredo evenly among four bowls and serve topped with more Parmesan and a sprinkling of fresh parsley.

INGREDIENTS:

2 boneless, skinless chicken breasts (about 1 lb)
8 oz whole wheat fettuccine
1 tablespoon olive oil
2 tablespoons unsalted butter
1 1/2 cups heavy cream
1 large egg yolk
2 large or 3 medium garlic cloves, minced
1 cup Parmesan, finely grated
Salt and pepper to taste
4 tablespoons of fresh parsley, chopped, for garnish (optional)

SERVES 4

*Yes, this is the full fat version, but it's so good I couldn't leave it out. **For a lighter sauce,** you can substitute heavy cream with milk and 1-2 tablespoons of cornstarch (whisk the cornstarch into the milk before adding).*

KALE PESTO PASTA

INGREDIENTS:

FOR THE KALE PESTO:
2 cups packed kale leaves, stems removed
1/2 cup Parmesan cheese, grated
1/3 cup pine nuts
2 cloves garlic, minced
1/2 cup extra-virgin olive oil
Salt and pepper to taste

FOR THE PASTA:
8 ounces whole grain pasta
Zest and juice of 1 lemon
Extra grated Parmesan cheese, for serving

SERVES 4

PREPARE THE KALE PESTO: In a food processor, combine the kale, Parmesan cheese, pine nuts, and garlic. Pulse until finely chopped. With the motor running, slowly drizzle in the olive oil until the mixture becomes a smooth paste. Season with salt and pepper to taste.

COOK THE PASTA: Bring a large pot of salted water to a boil. Add the pasta and cook according to the package instructions until al dente. Before draining, reserve 1/2 cup of the pasta water.

COMBINE THE PESTO AND PASTA: Drain the pasta and return it to the pot. Add the kale pesto and toss to coat, adding a little of the reserved pasta water if needed to thin the sauce.

SEASON AND SERVE: Stir in the lemon zest and juice. Taste and adjust the seasoning if necessary.

SERVE: Divide the pasta among four plates. Top with additional grated Parmesan cheese and serve immediately.

LEMON ASPARAGUS PASTA

COOK THE PASTA: Bring a large pot of salted water to a boil. Add the spaghetti and cook according to package instructions until al dente. During the last 2 minutes of cooking, add the cut asparagus to the pot. Once done, drain the pasta and asparagus, reserving about 1 cup of the pasta water.

PREPARE THE SAUCE: While the pasta is cooking, heat the olive oil in a large pan over medium heat. Add the minced garlic and cook until fragrant, about 1 minute. Stir in the lemon zest and juice.

COMBINE: Add the cooked pasta and asparagus to the pan with the garlic and lemon. Toss well to combine. If needed, add some of the reserved pasta water to help the sauce coat the pasta.

ADD CHEESE: Remove the pan from the heat and stir in the grated Parmesan cheese. Season with salt and pepper to taste.

SERVE: Divide the pasta among four plates. Garnish with fresh parsley and serve immediately.

INGREDIENTS:

8 ounces whole wheat spaghetti
1 pound asparagus, trimmed and cut into 1-inch pieces
2 tablespoons olive oil
3 cloves garlic, minced
Zest and juice of 1 lemon
1/2 cup Parmesan cheese, grated
Salt and pepper to taste
Fresh parsley, chopped, for garnish

SERVES 4

LINGUINE WITH CLAM SAUCE

INGREDIENTS:

8 ounces linguine
2 tablespoons olive oil
4 cloves garlic, minced
1/2 teaspoon crushed red pepper flakes
1 cup dry white wine
2 cans (6.5 ounces each) chopped clams, juice reserved
Salt and pepper to taste
Zest and juice of 1 lemon
1/4 cup fresh parsley, chopped
Parmesan cheese, grated, for serving

SERVES 4

COOK THE LINGUINE: Bring a large pot of salted water to a boil. Add the linguine and cook according to the package instructions until al dente. Drain and set aside.

SAUTÉ THE GARLIC: While the pasta is cooking, heat the olive oil in a large skillet over medium heat. Add the minced garlic and crushed red pepper flakes and sauté until fragrant, about 1 minute.

MAKE THE CLAM SAUCE: Add the white wine and reserved clam juice to the skillet. Bring to a boil and let it simmer for 5 minutes.

ADD THE CLAMS: Stir in the chopped clams, salt, and pepper, and cook until heated through, about 2 minutes.

COMBINE THE PASTA AND SAUCE: Add the cooked linguine to the skillet and toss until well coated in the sauce. Stir in the lemon zest, lemon juice, and fresh parsley.

SERVE: Divide the pasta among four plates. Top with grated Parmesan cheese and serve immediately.

ROASTED RED PEPPER PASTA

INGREDIENTS:

18 oz of whole grain spaghetti
2 large red bell peppers
2 tablespoons olive oil
2 garlic cloves, minced
1/2 cup of low-sodium vegetable broth
1/2 cup of Parmesan cheese, grated
Salt and pepper to taste
Fresh basil leaves for garnish

SERVES 4

ROAST THE PEPPERS: Preheat the oven to 400°F. Place the red bell peppers on a baking sheet and roast for about 20 minutes, or until the skin is charred and blistered. Let cool, then peel off the skin and remove the seeds.

COOK THE SPAGHETTI: Meanwhile, cook the spaghetti according to the package instructions. Drain and set aside, reserving 1 cup of the pasta water.

SAUTÉ THE GARLIC: In a large skillet, heat the olive oil over medium heat. Add the minced garlic and sauté until fragrant.

ADD THE ROASTED PEPPERS: Add the roasted red peppers to the skillet and cook for another 2 minutes.

PURÉE THE SAUCE: Pour the vegetable broth into the skillet, simmer for five minutes, then transfer the mixture to a blender or food processor. Blend until smooth.

COMBINE THE PASTA AND SAUCE: Return the sauce to the skillet and simmer over low heat. Add the cooked spaghetti and toss until well coated. If the sauce is too thick, add some of the reserved pasta water.

SEASON THE SAUCE: Stir in the Parmesan cheese and season with salt and pepper.

SERVE: Divide the pasta among four plates, garnish with fresh basil leaves, and serve.

SPICY SAUSAGE RIGATONI

INGREDIENTS:

8 ounces rigatoni
1 tablespoon olive oil
1/2 pound spicy Italian sausage, casings removed
1 small onion, chopped
2 cloves garlic, minced
1 can (14.5 ounces) diced tomatoes
1/2 teaspoon dried oregano
1/4 teaspoon red pepper flakes
Salt and pepper to taste
1/4 cup fresh basil, chopped
Parmesan cheese, grated, for serving

SERVES 4

COOK THE RIGATONI: Bring a large pot of salted water to a boil. Add the rigatoni and cook according to the package instructions until al dente. Drain and set aside.

SAUTÉ THE SAUSAGE: While the pasta is cooking, heat the olive oil in a large skillet over medium heat. Add the sausage and cook, breaking it up into crumbles with a spoon, until browned and cooked through, about 5-7 minutes.

SAUTÉ THE AROMATICS: Add the chopped onion and minced garlic to the skillet and sauté until the onion is softened, about 3 minutes.

MAKE THE SAUCE: Stir in the diced tomatoes, dried oregano, red pepper flakes, salt, and pepper. Let the sauce simmer for about 5 minutes to let the flavors meld together.

COMBINE THE PASTA AND SAUCE: Add the cooked rigatoni to the skillet and toss until well coated in the sauce.

SERVE: Divide the pasta among four plates. Top with chopped fresh basil and grated Parmesan cheese, and serve immediately.

SKILLET LASAGNA

INGREDIENTS:

1 tablespoon olive oil
1 pound lean turkey, ground
1 onion, diced
2 cloves of garlic, minced
1 cup marinara sauce
1 cup low-fat ricotta cheese
6 whole wheat lasagna noodles, broken into pieces
1 cup low-fat mozzarella cheese, shredded
1/4 cup Parmesan cheese, grated
Salt and pepper to taste
Fresh basil leaves, for garnish

SERVES 4

COOK THE TURKEY: In a large skillet, heat the olive oil over medium heat. Add the ground turkey, season with salt and pepper, and cook until browned. Remove the turkey from the skillet and set aside.

SAUTÉ THE AROMATICS: In the same skillet, sauté the diced onion until soft and translucent. Add the minced garlic and cook for another minute.

COMBINE INGREDIENTS: Return the cooked turkey to the skillet. Add the marinara sauce, ricotta cheese, and broken lasagna noodles. Stir to combine, ensuring that the noodles are covered in sauce. Cover the skillet and simmer for 10 minutes, or until the noodles are al dente.

ADD THE CHEESE: Sprinkle the mozzarella and Parmesan cheese over the top of the lasagna. Cover again and cook for another 2-3 minutes, until the cheese is melted and bubbly.

SERVE: Garnish with fresh basil leaves, and serve hot straight from the skillet.

SPAGHETTI AGLIO E OLIO

INGREDIENTS:

8 oz of whole grain spaghetti
1/3 cup extra virgin olive oil
6 large garlic cloves, thinly sliced
1/2 teaspoon red pepper flakes (adjust to taste)
Salt to taste
1/4 cup fresh parsley, chopped
Zest of 1 lemon
Freshly ground black pepper

SERVES 4

COOK THE SPAGHETTI: Cook the spaghetti in a large pot of boiling salted water until al dente, according to package instructions.

SAUTÉ THE GARLIC: While the pasta cooks, heat the olive oil in a large pan over medium heat. Add the sliced garlic and sauté until it just starts to brown.

ADD THE PEPPER FLAKES: Add the red pepper flakes to the garlic and oil, stir for about 30 seconds to infuse the oil with the spice.

COMBINE THE SAUCE AND SPAGHETTI: Using tongs, transfer the cooked spaghetti directly from the pot to the pan with the garlic oil, letting some pasta water drip into the pan as well.

TOSS AND COAT THE SPAGHETTI: Toss everything together for about 2 minutes until the spaghetti is well coated in the garlic oil. If it seems dry, add a bit more pasta water.

GARNISH: Remove from heat, then add the chopped parsley, lemon zest, and a generous amount of black pepper. Toss well to combine.

SERVE: Taste and adjust salt if necessary. Serve immediately with extra red pepper flakes on the side.

SPAGHETTI CARBONARA

COOK THE SPAGHETTI: Cook the spaghetti according to the package instructions until al dente. Drain the pasta, reserving about 1 cup of the pasta water.

SAUTÉ THE GARLIC AND BACON: While the pasta is cooking, heat the olive oil in a large skillet over medium heat. Add the garlic and turkey bacon and sauté until the bacon is crispy, about 4-5 minutes.

PREPARE THE EGG MIXTURE: In a separate bowl, whisk together the eggs and Parmesan cheese. Season with a little salt and plenty of black pepper.

COMBINE: Once the spaghetti is cooked and drained, immediately add it to the skillet with the bacon. Toss well to coat in the bacon fat.

ADD THE EGG MIXTURE: Remove the skillet from the heat. Pour the egg mixture over the pasta, and quickly toss everything together until the pasta is evenly coated and creamy. If it's too thick, add a bit of the reserved pasta water.

SERVE: Sprinkle with fresh parsley before serving. Serve immediately.

INGREDIENTS:

8 oz of whole wheat spaghetti
1 tablespoon of olive oil
4 cloves of garlic, minced
6 slices of turkey bacon, diced
2 large eggs
1/2 cup of grated Parmesan cheese
Salt and black pepper to taste
A handful of fresh parsley, chopped

SERVES 4

APPLE CIDER PORK CHOPS

INGREDIENTS:

4 boneless pork chops, about 1 inch thick
Salt and pepper to taste
1 tablespoon olive oil
1 medium onion, thinly sliced
2 cloves garlic, minced
1 teaspoon fresh thyme, chopped
1/2 cup apple cider
1/2 cup low-sodium chicken broth
2 tablespoons Dijon mustard
2 apples, cored and sliced

SERVES 4

PREPARE THE PORK CHOPS: Season the pork chops on both sides with salt and pepper.

SEAR THE CHOPS: Heat the olive oil in a large skillet over medium-high heat. Add the pork chops and sear until browned on both sides, about 3-4 minutes per side. Remove the pork chops from the skillet and set aside.

SAUTÉ THE AROMATICS In the same skillet, add the onion, garlic, and thyme. Sauté until the onion is softened and starts to brown, about 5 minutes.

MAKE THE SAUCE: Stir in the apple cider, chicken broth, and Dijon mustard. Bring the mixture to a simmer, scraping up any browned bits from the bottom of the skillet.

COMBINE THE PORK CHOPS AND APPLES: Return the pork chops to the skillet and add the sliced apples. Cook for another 5-7 minutes, or until the pork chops are cooked through and the apples are tender.

SERVE: Serve the pork chops hot, with the apple and onion mixture spooned over the top.

SMOKED SAUSAGE SKILLET

COOK THE SAUSAGE: Heat 1 tablespoon of the olive oil in a large skillet over medium heat. Add the smoked sausage rounds and cook until browned on both sides, about 5-7 minutes. Remove the sausage from the skillet and set aside.

SAUTÉ THE VEGETABLES: In the same skillet, add the remaining tablespoon of olive oil, followed by the chopped onion, minced garlic, diced bell pepper, and diced zucchinis. Cook until the vegetables are tender, about 5-7 minutes.

ADD THE TOMATOES AND SPICES: Add the drained diced tomatoes to the skillet, followed by the dried oregano, smoked paprika, salt, and pepper. Stir well to combine.

COMBINE: Return the cooked sausage to the skillet and stir well to combine with the vegetables and spices. Allow the mixture to simmer for a few minutes until everything is heated through.

SERVE: Divide the smoked sausage skillet between four plates. Garnish with chopped fresh parsley before serving.

INGREDIENTS:

1 lb smoked sausage, sliced into rounds
2 tablespoons olive oil
1 onion, chopped
2 cloves garlic, minced
1 bell pepper, diced
2 zucchinis, diced
1 can (14.5 oz) diced tomatoes, drained
1 teaspoon dried oregano
1 teaspoon smoked paprika
Salt and pepper to taste
Fresh parsley, chopped, for garnish

SERVES 4

Serve over brown rice or quinoa (or any grain of your choice!) to round out this quick, flavorful dish.

AUTHOR'S NOTE

SWEET AND SOUR PORK

INGREDIENTS:

1 lb lean pork tenderloin, cut into bite-sized pieces
Salt and pepper to taste
2 tablespoons olive oil, divided
1 bell pepper, chopped
1 medium onion, chopped
1 carrot, thinly sliced
1 can (8 oz) pineapple chunks in juice, drained and juice reserved
1/4 cup apple cider vinegar
2 tablespoons honey
1 tablespoon cornstarch
2 tablespoons low-sodium soy sauce
2 green onions, sliced for garnish

SERVES 4

PREPARE THE PORK: Season the pork pieces with salt and pepper.

COOK THE PORK: In a large skillet, heat 1 tablespoon of the olive oil over medium-high heat. Add the pork and stir-fry until browned and cooked through, about 5-7 minutes. Transfer the pork to a plate and set it aside.

COOK THE VEGETABLES: In the same skillet, add the remaining 1 tablespoon of olive oil. Add the bell pepper, onion, and carrot, and stir-fry until they are tender-crisp, about 3-4 minutes. Add the pineapple chunks and cook for another minute.

MAKE THE SAUCE: In a small bowl, whisk together the reserved pineapple juice, apple cider vinegar, honey, cornstarch, and soy sauce until smooth.

COMBINE AND SIMMER: Return the pork to the skillet. Pour the sauce over the pork and vegetables. Stir everything together and let it simmer for about 2-3 minutes, or until the sauce has thickened.

SERVE: Divide between four plates. Sprinkle with green onions, and serve immediately.

CAPRESE PASTA SALAD

COOK THE PASTA: Cook the pasta according to the package instructions until al dente. Drain and rinse under cold water to cool.

COMBINE THE REMAINING INGREDIENTS: In a large bowl, combine the cooled pasta, cherry tomatoes, mozzarella, and basil leaves.

MAKE THE DRESSING: In a small bowl, whisk together the olive oil, balsamic vinegar, salt, and pepper.

TOSS THE SALAD: Pour the dressing over the pasta mixture and toss until well combined. Adjust the seasoning if necessary.

SERVE: Let the salad rest for 10 minutes to allow the flavors to meld together. You can also refrigerate it for later use. Serve chilled or at room temperature.

INGREDIENTS:

8 oz whole wheat pasta (penne or farfalle work great)
1 pint cherry tomatoes, halved
8 oz fresh mozzarella balls, halved (or cubed larger mozzarella)
1/2 cup fresh basil leaves, torn or chopped
3 tablespoons olive oil
2 tablespoons balsamic vinegar
Salt and pepper to taste

SERVES 4

CHICKEN CAESAR SALAD

PREPARE THE CHICKEN: Season the chicken breasts with salt and pepper. Heat the olive oil in a grill pan over medium heat. Add the chicken and cook for 6-7 minutes on each side, or until cooked through and no longer pink in the middle. Remove from heat and let rest for a few minutes, then slice into thin strips.

MAKE THE CAESAR DRESSING: In a small bowl, combine the minced garlic, Greek yogurt, lemon juice, Worcestershire sauce, and grated parmesan. Season with salt and pepper, and whisk until well blended.

ASSEMBLE THE SALAD: In a large bowl, toss the chopped romaine lettuce with the Caesar dressing until well coated. Divide the salad among four plates. Top each serving with a portion of the grilled chicken strips and a sprinkle of whole grain croutons.

SERVE: Garnish with shaved parmesan, and serve immediately.

INGREDIENTS:

2 boneless, skinless chicken breasts
Salt and pepper to taste
1 tablespoon olive oil
2 heads of romaine lettuce, chopped
1/2 cup whole grain croutons
Parmesan cheese, shaved, for garnish

FOR THE CAESAR DRESSING:

2 cloves garlic, minced
1/2 cup Greek yogurt
1 tablespoon lemon juice
1 tablespoon Worcestershire sauce
1/4 cup parmesan cheese, grated
Salt and pepper to taste

SERVES 4

GREEK COUSCOUS SALAD

COOK THE COUSCOUS: Prepare the couscous according to package instructions. Once cooked, fluff it with a fork and let it cool slightly.

PREPARE THE SALAD: In a large bowl, combine the cooled couscous, halved cherry tomatoes, diced cucumber, diced red bell pepper, sliced Kalamata olives, crumbled feta cheese, chopped parsley, and chopped mint.

MAKE THE DRESSING: In a small bowl, whisk together the lemon juice, extra virgin olive oil, salt, and pepper to create the vinaigrette.

DRESS THE SALAD: Pour the vinaigrette over the couscous salad and toss to combine, ensuring that all ingredients are evenly coated.

SERVE: Divide the salad among four plates. It can be served immediately, or refrigerated for an hour to allow the flavors to meld together.

INGREDIENTS:

1 cup dry couscous
1 cup cherry tomatoes, halved
1 cucumber, diced
1 red bell pepper, diced
1/2 cup Kalamata olives, pitted and sliced
1/2 cup feta cheese, crumbled
1/4 cup fresh parsley, chopped
1/4 cup fresh mint, chopped
Juice of 1 lemon
1/4 cup extra virgin olive oil
Salt and pepper to taste

SERVES 4

If you are in the mood for something heartier, add grilled chicken, salmon or roasted vegetables for additional depth of flavor. Any protein of your choice works well with this versatile salad!

AUTHOR'S NOTE

QUINOA SALAD WITH GRILLED CHICKEN

INGREDIENTS:

1 cup uncooked quinoa
2 cups water
2 boneless, skinless chicken breasts
1 tablespoon olive oil
Salt and pepper to taste
1 cup cherry tomatoes, halved
1 cucumber, diced
1/4 cup fresh parsley, chopped
1/4 cup fresh mint, chopped

FOR THE LEMON VINAIGRETTE:
Juice of 1 large lemon
1/3 cup extra virgin olive oil
1 clove garlic, minced
Salt and pepper to taste

SERVES 4

COOK THE QUINOA: In a medium pot, bring the quinoa and water to a boil. Reduce the heat to low, cover, and let it simmer for 15 minutes or until the quinoa is cooked and fluffy. Once done, set aside to cool.

PREPARE THE CHICKEN: While the quinoa is cooking, season the chicken breasts with olive oil, salt, and pepper. Grill over medium heat for 6-7 minutes per side, or until fully cooked. Allow the chicken to rest for a few minutes, then cut into thin slices.

PREPARE THE VINAIGRETTE: In a small bowl, whisk together the lemon juice, olive oil, and minced garlic. Season with salt and pepper to taste.

ASSEMBLE THE SALAD: In a large bowl, combine the cooled quinoa, sliced chicken, cherry tomatoes, cucumber, parsley, and mint. Pour the vinaigrette over the salad and toss everything together until well combined.

SERVE: Divide the salad among four plates, and serve immediately.

TUNA NIÇOISE

INGREDIENTS:

2 cans of tuna in olive oil
4 small potatoes, washed and halved
2 cups of green beans, ends trimmed
4 eggs
2 cups of mixed salad greens
1 cup of cherry tomatoes, halved
1/4 cup of pitted black olives
1 small red onion, thinly sliced
2 tablespoons of olive oil
1 tablespoon of Dijon mustard
2 tablespoons of white wine vinegar
Salt and pepper to taste

SERVES 4

COOK THE POTATOES AND EGGS: Place the potatoes in a pot of salted water, bring to a boil and cook for 10-15 minutes until tender. In the last 3 minutes of cooking, add the green beans.
In another pot, bring water to a boil, gently add the eggs, and boil for 6-7 minutes for a slightly soft center.

MAKE THE DRESSING: As the potatoes and eggs are cooking, prepare the dressing by whisking together the olive oil, Dijon mustard, white wine vinegar, and salt and pepper to taste.

DRAIN AND COOL THE POTATOES: Drain the potatoes and green beans and run them under cold water to cool.

PEEL THE EGGS: Peel and halve the eggs.

COMBINE THE INGREDIENTS: Assemble the salad by dividing the salad greens among 4 plates. Top with the potatoes, green beans, tuna, cherry tomatoes, olives, eggs, and onion slices.

SERVE: Drizzle the dressing over the top of each salad and serve.

EGG DROP SOUP

HEAT THE BROTH: In a large pot, bring the chicken broth to a boil over medium-high heat.

ADD THE VEGGIES: Add the frozen peas and carrots mix, soy sauce, and grated ginger to the pot. Stir well and let it simmer for about 3 minutes, or until the veggies are cooked through.

CREATE THE EGG RIBBONS: Slowly drizzle the beaten eggs into the boiling broth, stirring constantly to create thin ribbons of egg.

SEASON THE SOUP: Season with salt and pepper to taste.

SERVE: Ladle the soup into bowls, top with the sliced green onions, and serve hot.

INGREDIENTS:

4 cups low-sodium chicken broth
2 eggs, beaten
1/2 cup frozen peas and carrots mix
2 green onions, sliced
1 teaspoon soy sauce
1/2 teaspoon fresh ginger, grated
Salt and pepper to taste

SERVES 4

LENTIL AND TOMATO SOUP

SAUTÉ THE VEGETABLES: Heat the olive oil in a large pot over medium heat. Add the diced onion and cook until it's softened and translucent, about 5 minutes. Add the minced garlic, dried oregano, dried basil, salt, and pepper, and cook until fragrant, about 1 minute.

ADD THE TOMATOES, BROTH, AND LENTILS: Add the diced tomatoes, vegetable broth, and lentils to the pot. Stir to combine and bring the mixture to a boil.

SIMMER THE SOUP: Reduce the heat to low and let the soup simmer for about 15 minutes, or until the lentils are tender.

FINISH THE SOUP: Stir in the balsamic vinegar and taste the soup. Adjust the seasoning if necessary.

SERVE: Ladle the soup into bowls, garnish with fresh basil, and serve hot.

INGREDIENTS:

1 tablespoon olive oil
1 onion, diced
2 cloves garlic, minced
1 teaspoon dried oregano
1 teaspoon dried basil
Salt and pepper to taste
1 can (14.5 ounces) diced tomatoes
4 cups vegetable broth
1 cup dried red lentils
1 tablespoon balsamic vinegar
Fresh basil, torn, for garnish

SERVES 4

RAMEN NOODLE SOUP

PREPARE THE BROTH: In a large pot, bring the chicken broth and water to a boil.

SEASON AND ADD THE VEGETABLES: Add in the soy sauce, sesame oil, garlic, ginger, and mixed vegetables. Lower the heat and let it simmer for about 10 minutes until the vegetables are tender.

COOK THE NOODLES: In another pot, cook the ramen noodles according to the package instructions, then drain and set aside.

COMBINE AND SEASON: Add the cooked ramen noodles, green onions, and shredded chicken to the soup pot. Stir until everything is well combined and heated through. Season with salt and pepper to taste.

SERVE: Serve the soup hot, garnished with fresh cilantro and lime wedges on the side.

INGREDIENTS:

2 packs of ramen noodles, seasoning packets discarded
4 cups of low-sodium chicken broth
2 cups of water
2 tablespoons of soy sauce
1 tablespoon of sesame oil
2 cloves of garlic, minced
1-inch piece of fresh ginger, grated
2 cups of mixed vegetables (carrots, bell peppers, mushrooms, etc.), chopped
2 green onions, chopped
1 cup of cooked chicken, shredded
Salt and pepper to taste
Fresh cilantro and lime wedges for serving

SERVES 4

ROASTED RED PEPPER SOUP

INGREDIENTS:

4 red bell peppers
1 tablespoon olive oil
1 onion, diced
2 cloves garlic, minced
1 can (14 oz) diced tomatoes
3 cups vegetable broth
1/2 cup fresh basil leaves
1/2 cup plain Greek yogurt
Salt and pepper to taste

SERVES 4

ROAST THE PEPPERS: Preheat your oven to 425°F and line a baking sheet with parchment paper. Place the bell peppers on the sheet and roast for about 25-30 minutes, or until the skin is blistered and charred. Remove from the oven and let them cool.

PREPARE THE SOUP BASE: While the peppers are cooling, heat the olive oil in a large pot over medium heat. Add the onion and garlic, and sauté until the onion is translucent.

PEEL AND CHOP THE PEPPERS: Once the peppers are cool enough to handle, peel off the skin, remove the seeds and chop them.

COOK THE SOUP: Add the chopped peppers, diced tomatoes, and vegetable broth to the pot. Bring to a boil, then reduce heat and simmer for about 10 minutes.

BLEND THE SOUP: Using an immersion blender (or in batches in a countertop blender), blend the soup until smooth.

FINISH AND SERVE: Stir in the fresh basil leaves and Greek yogurt, and season with salt and pepper to taste. Serve hot, garnished with a dollop of Greek yogurt or a few small basil leaves.

SAUSAGE AND WHITE BEAN STEW

BROWN THE SAUSAGE: Heat the olive oil in a large pot over medium-high heat. Add the sliced sausage and cook until browned, about 5-7 minutes. Remove the sausage with a slotted spoon and set aside.

SAUTÉ THE VEGETABLES: In the same pot, add the diced onion and carrots. Cook until the vegetables are softened, about 5 minutes. Add the minced garlic, thyme, salt, and pepper, and cook until fragrant, about 1 minute.

ADD THE BROTH AND BEANS: Add the chicken broth and white beans to the pot. Stir to combine, then bring the mixture to a boil.

SIMMER THE STEW: Reduce the heat to low, return the sausage to the pot, and add the chopped kale. Cover the pot and let the stew simmer for about 10 minutes, until the kale is wilted and the flavors are melded together.

FINISH THE STEW: Remove the pot from the heat and stir in the lemon juice. Taste and adjust the seasoning if necessary.

SERVE: Ladle the stew into bowls and garnish with fresh parsley. Serve hot.

INGREDIENTS:

1 tablespoon olive oil
1 pound smoked sausage, sliced
1 onion, diced
2 carrots, diced
2 cloves garlic, minced
1 teaspoon dried thyme
Salt and pepper to taste
4 cups chicken broth
2 cans (15 ounces each) white beans, drained and rinsed
4 cups kale, roughly chopped
1 tablespoon lemon juice
Fresh parsley, chopped, for garnish

SERVES 4

TACO SOUP

INGREDIENTS:

1 lb lean ground beef or turkey
1 large onion, diced
2 cloves garlic, minced
1 packet (1 oz) taco seasoning
1 can (15 oz) black beans, drained and rinsed
1 can (15 oz) whole kernel corn, drained
1 can (10 oz) diced tomatoes with green chilies
(like Rotel)
1 can (8 oz) tomato sauce
2 cups low-sodium chicken broth
Toppings: shredded cheese, sour cream,
chopped fresh cilantro, sliced avocado

SERVES 4

BROWN THE BEEF: In a large pot, brown the ground beef or turkey over medium heat. Drain off any excess fat.

ADD THE AROMATICS: Add the diced onion to the pot and cook until translucent. Add the garlic and cook for another minute until fragrant.

ADD THE SEASONING: Stir in the taco seasoning to evenly coat the meat and onions.

ADD THE REMAINING INGREDIENTS: Add the beans, corn, diced tomatoes with chilies, tomato sauce, and chicken broth. Stir to combine.

COOK THE SOUP: Increase the heat to bring the mixture to a boil, then reduce the heat and let it simmer for 10-15 minutes to let the flavors meld together.

FINISH AND SERVE: Serve the soup hot, garnished with your choice of shredded cheese, sour cream, chopped fresh cilantro, and avocado slices.

TURKEY AND BEAN CHILI

SAUTÉ THE TURKEY: Heat the olive oil in a large pot over medium heat. Add the ground turkey and cook until browned and cooked through, about 5-7 minutes.

ADD THE AROMATICS: Add the chopped onion and minced garlic to the pot. Cook until the onion is softened, about 3 minutes.

ADD THE BEANS, TOMATOES, AND SPICES: Add the kidney beans, diced tomatoes with juice, chili powder, ground cumin, salt, and pepper to the pot. Stir to combine.

SIMMER THE CHILI: Pour in the chicken broth and bring the mixture to a boil. Reduce the heat to low and let the chili simmer for about 10 minutes.

SERVE: Ladle the chili into bowls. Garnish with chopped fresh cilantro and serve with lime wedges on the side.

INGREDIENTS:

1 tablespoon olive oil
1 pound lean ground turkey
1 onion, chopped
2 cloves garlic, minced
1 can (15 ounces) kidney beans, drained and rinsed
1 can (14.5 ounces) diced tomatoes, with juice
2 tablespoons chili powder
1 teaspoon ground cumin
Salt and pepper to taste
1 cup low-sodium chicken broth
Fresh cilantro, chopped, for garnish
Lime wedges, for serving

SERVES 4

CHICKPEA AND SPINACH CURRY

SAUTÉ THE AROMATICS: Heat the olive oil in a large pan over medium heat. Add the chopped onion and cook until it starts to soften, about 3-5 minutes. Add the minced garlic, grated ginger, curry powder, ground cumin, and turmeric. Stir well and cook for another minute until the spices are fragrant.

ADD THE CHICKPEAS AND TOMATOES: Add the drained and rinsed chickpeas and the canned diced tomatoes (with their juice) to the pan. Stir well to combine with the onion and spices.

ADD THE SPINACH AND COCONUT MILK: Add the fresh spinach to the pan, followed by the coconut milk. Stir well and bring the mixture to a simmer. Cook for about 5-10 minutes, until the spinach has wilted and the curry has thickened slightly.

SEASON: Taste the curry and add salt and pepper as needed.

SERVE: Divide the curry among four bowls. Garnish with fresh cilantro and serve with a lemon wedge on the side.

INGREDIENTS:

2 tablespoons olive oil
1 onion, finely chopped
3 cloves garlic, minced
1 tablespoon fresh ginger, grated
1 tablespoon curry powder
1 teaspoon ground cumin
1/2 teaspoon turmeric
1 can (14 oz) chickpeas, drained and rinsed
1 can (14 oz) diced tomatoes
2 cups fresh spinach
1 cup coconut milk
Salt and pepper to taste
Chopped fresh cilantro and lemon wedges, for garnish

SERVES 4

EGG SALAD SANDWICHES

PREPARE THE EGG SALAD: Chop the hard-boiled eggs and place them in a large bowl. Add the Greek yogurt, Dijon mustard, chopped celery, and chives. Season with salt and pepper to taste. Gently mix everything together until well combined.

ASSEMBLE THE SANDWICHES: Lay out 4 slices of whole grain bread. Divide the egg salad equally among the slices. Top each with lettuce and tomato slices, and then with the remaining slices of bread.

SERVE: Cut each sandwich in half, if desired, and serve immediately.

INGREDIENTS:

8 hard-boiled eggs, peeled
1/4 cup plain Greek yogurt
2 tablespoons Dijon mustard
1/4 cup celery, finely chopped
2 tablespoons fresh chives, finely chopped
Salt and pepper to taste
8 slices of whole grain bread
Lettuce and tomato slices, for serving

SERVES 4

EGGPLANT PARMESAN

INGREDIENTS:

1 medium eggplant, sliced into 1/2-inch thick rounds
Salt and pepper to taste
1/2 cup whole wheat flour
2 eggs, beaten
1 cup whole wheat breadcrumbs
1 cup marinara sauce
1 cup low-fat mozzarella cheese, shredded
1/4 cup Parmesan cheese, grated
Fresh basil leaves, for garnish

SERVES 4

PREHEAT THE OVEN: Preheat your oven to 425°F and line a baking sheet with parchment paper.

PREPARE THE EGGPLANT: Season the eggplant slices with salt and pepper. Dredge each slice in flour, dip into the beaten eggs, and then coat in breadcrumbs. Place the coated slices on the prepared baking sheet.

BAKE THE EGGPLANT: Bake for 15 minutes, flipping halfway through, until the eggplant slices are golden and crispy.

ASSEMBLE THE DISH: Spread a thin layer of marinara sauce on each eggplant slice, followed by a sprinkle of mozzarella and Parmesan cheese.

BROIL: Switch the oven to broil and return the baking sheet to the oven. Broil for 2-3 minutes, or until the cheese is bubbly and slightly browned.

SERVE: Garnish with fresh basil leaves, and serve hot.

ENCHILADAS

INGREDIENTS:

1 tablespoon olive oil
1 small onion, chopped
2 cloves garlic, minced
1 can (15 oz) black beans, drained and rinsed
1 cup frozen corn, thawed
2 cups enchilada sauce (recipe below)
8 small whole wheat tortillas
1 cup low-fat cheese, shredded
Fresh cilantro, chopped, for garnish

FOR THE ENCHILADA SAUCE:
2 cups low-sodium vegetable broth
3 tablespoons chili powder
1 tablespoon cumin
2 tablespoons flour
Salt to taste

SERVES 4

PREHEAT THE OVEN: Preheat your oven to 400°F.

PREPARE THE FILLING: In a large skillet, heat the olive oil over medium heat. Add the chopped onion and minced garlic, and sauté until the onion is translucent. Add the black beans and corn, and cook for another 2-3 minutes until heated through.

MAKE THE ENCHILADA SAUCE: In a medium saucepan, whisk together the vegetable broth, chili powder, cumin, and flour. Bring to a boil, then reduce to a simmer. Cook until the sauce thickens, about 5 minutes. Season with salt to taste.

ASSEMBLE THE ENCHILADAS: Spread a thin layer of enchilada sauce in the bottom of a baking dish. Fill each tortilla with the bean and corn mixture, roll tightly, and place seam-side down in the dish. Repeat with the remaining tortillas. Pour the rest of the enchilada sauce over the top, and sprinkle with the shredded cheese.

BAKE THE ENCHILADAS: Bake for 10-12 minutes, or until the cheese is melted and bubbly.

SERVE: Garnish with fresh cilantro, and serve hot.

This recipe also works great with chicken, shredded pork, asada or roasted vegetables.

AUTHOR'S NOTE

FALAFEL WRAPS WITH TZATZIKI

PREPARE THE FALAFEL MIXTURE: In a food processor, combine the chickpeas, onion, garlic, cumin, coriander, salt, pepper, and flour. Process until you have a coarse mixture that holds together when pressed.

FORM AND COOK THE FALAFELS: Divide the mixture into 8 equal portions and shape each portion into a patty. Heat the olive oil in a large pan over medium heat. Add the falafel patties and cook until browned on both sides, about 3 minutes per side.

PREPARE THE TZATZIKI: While the falafels are cooking, make the tzatziki. In a bowl, combine the Greek yogurt, grated cucumber, garlic, dill, lemon juice, and salt. Stir until well combined.

ASSEMBLE THE WRAPS: Warm the pita breads in the oven or on the stovetop. On each pita, spread a generous amount of tzatziki, then add lettuce, tomato, cucumber, and two falafel patties.

SERVE: Fold the pita bread over the fillings and serve the wraps immediately.

SERVES 4

INGREDIENTS:

FOR THE FALAFEL:
1 can (15 ounces) chickpeas, drained and rinsed
1/2 large onion, roughly chopped
2 cloves garlic, minced
2 teaspoons ground cumin
1 teaspoon ground coriander
Salt and pepper to taste
2 tablespoons all-purpose flour
2 tablespoons olive oil

FOR THE TZATZIKI:
1 cup Greek yogurt
1/2 cucumber, peeled and grated
1 clove garlic, minced
1 tablespoon fresh dill, chopped
Juice of 1/2 lemon
Salt to taste

FOR THE WRAPS:
4 pita breads
1 cup lettuce, shredded
1 tomato, sliced
1/2 cucumber, sliced

HUMMUS AND VEGGIE WRAPS

PREPARE THE TORTILLAS: Lay out the whole grain tortillas and spread an even layer of hummus on each.

ASSEMBLE THE WRAPS: On one side of the tortilla, arrange a layer of red bell pepper, cucumber, carrot, and avocado slices. Top with a handful of baby spinach.

SEASON: Sprinkle a little salt and pepper over the vegetables.

SERVE: Roll up the tortilla tightly, starting from the side with the vegetables. Slice in half and serve immediately, or wrap in foil for a portable meal.

INGREDIENTS:

4 whole grain tortillas
1 cup of hummus
1 red bell pepper, thinly sliced
1 cucumber, thinly sliced
1 carrot, peeled and thinly sliced
1 avocado, sliced
1 cup of baby spinach leaves
Salt and pepper to taste

SERVES 4

LOADED VEGETABLE QUESADILLAS

INGREDIENTS:

8 medium whole wheat tortillas
1 medium red bell pepper, thinly sliced
1 medium green bell pepper, thinly sliced
1 medium red onion, thinly sliced
1 medium zucchini, thinly sliced
2 cloves garlic, minced
2 cups reduced-fat Mexican cheese blend, shredded
1 tablespoon olive oil
1/2 teaspoon cumin
1/2 teaspoon chili powder
Salt and pepper to taste
Fresh cilantro for garnish
Salsa and Greek yogurt (as healthier alternative to sour cream), for serving

SERVES 4

SAUTÉ THE VEGETABLES: Heat the olive oil in a large skillet over medium heat. Add the bell peppers, red onion, zucchini, and garlic. Stir in the cumin and chili powder. Sauté for about 5-7 minutes, until the vegetables are just softened. Season with salt and pepper to taste.

PREPARE THE TORTILLAS: Lay out four tortillas on a clean surface. Distribute half of the cheese evenly among the tortillas, followed by the cooked vegetables, and then the remaining cheese. Top with the remaining four tortillas.

COOK THE QUESADILLAS: Wipe out the skillet and return it to medium heat. Cook each quesadilla for about 2-3 minutes per side, until the tortillas are golden and crispy, and the cheese is melted.

SERVE: Cut the quesadillas into quarters and serve warm with salsa and Greek yogurt on the side. Garnish with fresh cilantro.

MARGHERITA PIZZA

PREHEAT THE OVEN: Preheat your oven to 450°F. If you have a pizza stone, place it in the oven while preheating.

PREPARE THE PIZZA: Place the pizza crust on a pizza peel or an inverted baking sheet. Brush the crust evenly with the olive oil. Arrange the tomato slices over the crust, then sprinkle the mozzarella cheese on top. Season with a bit of salt and pepper.

BAKE THE PIZZA: Transfer the pizza to the preheated oven (or onto the preheated pizza stone if using) and bake for about 10-12 minutes, or until the cheese is melted and bubbly and the crust is golden.

GARNISH THE PIZZA: Remove the pizza from the oven. Scatter the fresh basil leaves over the hot pizza.

SERVE: Slice the pizza into wedges and serve immediately.

INGREDIENTS:

1 pre-made whole wheat pizza crust (about 12 inches)
1 tablespoon olive oil
1 large ripe tomato, thinly sliced
1 cup mozzarella cheese, shredded
1/2 cup fresh basil leaves
Salt and pepper to taste

SERVES 4

QUICHE LORRAINE

INGREDIENTS:

1 ready-made whole wheat pastry crust
4 strips of low-sodium bacon, chopped
1/2 onion, diced
5 eggs, beaten
1 cup low-fat milk
1 cup reduced-fat cheddar cheese, shredded
Salt and pepper to taste
Fresh chives, chopped, for garnish

SERVES 4

PREHEAT THE OVEN: Preheat your oven to 375°F and place the ready-made crust on a baking sheet.

COOK THE BACON AND ONION: In a skillet over medium heat, cook the bacon until crispy. Remove the bacon and set aside, leaving about a tablespoon of fat in the pan. Add the diced onion to the pan and sauté until softened and translucent.

PREPARE THE EGG MIXTURE: In a large bowl, combine the beaten eggs, milk, shredded cheese, cooked bacon, and sautéed onion. Season with salt and pepper and mix until well combined.

FILL THE CRUST: Pour the egg mixture into the prepared crust, making sure the filling is evenly distributed.

BAKE THE QUICHE: Bake for 15 minutes, or until the filling is set and the crust is golden.

SERVE: Allow the quiche to cool for a few minutes before slicing. Garnish with fresh chives, and serve warm.

QUINOA FRIED "RICE"

COOK THE QUINOA: Rinse the quinoa under cold water until the water runs clear. Combine the quinoa and broth in a medium saucepan. Bring to a boil, then reduce heat to low, cover, and simmer until quinoa is tender and the broth is absorbed, about 15 minutes. Set aside.

SAUTÉ THE ONION: In a large skillet or wok, heat the olive oil over medium heat. Add the onion and garlic and sauté until the onion is translucent, about 5 minutes.

ADD THE VEGETABLES: Stir in the frozen peas and carrots and cook until they are warmed through, about 5 minutes.

ADD THE EGGS: Push the vegetables to one side of the skillet and pour the beaten eggs onto the other side. Scramble the eggs, breaking them into small pieces with a spatula as they cook.

ADD THE QUINOA: Stir the cooked quinoa into the vegetable and egg mixture. Pour the soy sauce over the top and stir to combine. Cook for an additional 2 minutes to heat through.

FINISH AND SERVE: Season with salt and pepper to taste, then garnish with the chopped green onions before serving.

INGREDIENTS:

1 cup quinoa
2 cups low sodium chicken or vegetable broth
2 tablespoons olive oil
1 small onion, finely chopped
2 cloves garlic, minced
1 cup frozen peas and carrots
2 eggs, lightly beaten
3 tablespoons low-sodium soy sauce or tamari for gluten-free
2 green onions, chopped
Salt and pepper to taste

SERVES 4

QUINOA STUFFED PEPPERS

INGREDIENTS:

4 large bell peppers (a mix of colors)
1 cup quinoa
2 cups low-sodium vegetable broth
1 tablespoon olive oil
1 small onion, finely chopped
2 cloves garlic, minced
1 can (15 oz) black beans, drained and rinsed
1 can (14.5 oz) diced tomatoes
1 teaspoon cumin
1/2 teaspoon chili powder
Salt and pepper to taste
1/2 cup cheddar cheese, shredded
Fresh parsley or cilantro, chopped, for garnish

SERVES 4

PREHEAT THE OVEN AND PREPARE THE PEPPERS: Preheat your oven to 375°F. Cut the tops off the peppers, remove the seeds, and place them in a baking dish.

COOK THE QUINOA: In a medium saucepan, bring the vegetable broth to a boil. Add the quinoa, reduce the heat to low, cover, and let it simmer for 15 minutes, or until all the broth is absorbed.

SAUTÉ THE AROMATICS: While the quinoa is cooking, heat the olive oil in a skillet over medium heat. Add the onion and garlic, and sauté until the onion is translucent, about 5 minutes.

COMBINE THE FILLING: In a large bowl, combine the cooked quinoa, sautéed onion and garlic, black beans, diced tomatoes, cumin, chili powder, salt, and pepper. Stir everything together until well mixed.

STUFF THE PEPPERS: Divide the quinoa mixture between the bell peppers, packing it down as you fill them. Top each pepper with a sprinkle of cheddar cheese.

BAKE: Cover the baking dish with aluminum foil and bake for 25-30 minutes. Then, remove the foil and bake for another 5-10 minutes, or until the cheese is bubbly and slightly browned.

SERVE: Garnish with fresh parsley or cilantro, and serve hot.

This recipe takes a little longer than 30 minutes but is worth the wait!.

AUTHOR'S NOTE

RAINBOW VEGETABLE STIR-FRY

INGREDIENTS:

2 tablespoons olive oil
1 block firm tofu, drained and cut into cubes
Salt and pepper to taste
1 red bell pepper, thinly sliced
1 yellow bell pepper, thinly sliced
1 cup broccoli florets
2 carrots, peeled and thinly sliced
1 cup snap peas, ends trimmed
1 zucchini, thinly sliced
2 cloves garlic, minced
1 tablespoon fresh ginger, grated
3 tablespoons low-sodium soy sauce
2 tablespoons rice vinegar
1 tablespoon cornstarch mixed with 1 tablespoon water
2 green onions, chopped for garnish
Toasted sesame seeds, for garnish

SERVES 4

COOK THE TOFU: Heat 1 tablespoon of olive oil in a large pan or wok over medium-high heat. Add the tofu cubes, season with salt and pepper, and cook until browned on all sides, about 5-7 minutes. Remove the tofu from the pan and set aside.

STIR-FRY THE VEGETABLES: In the same pan, add the remaining tablespoon of olive oil. Add the sliced peppers, broccoli, carrots, snap peas, and zucchini. Stir-fry over high heat until the vegetables are just tender, about 5 minutes.

ADD THE GARLIC AND GINGER: Lower the heat to medium and add the minced garlic and grated ginger to the pan. Stir well and cook until fragrant, about 1 minute.

MAKE THE SAUCE: Add the soy sauce and rice vinegar to the pan. Stir well to coat the vegetables. Then, add the cornstarch-water mixture to thicken the sauce. Stir continuously for about 1 minute until the sauce has thickened.

COMBINE: Return the cooked tofu to the pan and stir well to combine with the vegetables and sauce.

SERVE: Divide the stir-fry among four plates. Garnish with chopped green onions and sesame seeds before serving.

RATATOUILLE WITH POLENTA

INGREDIENTS:

1 cup instant polenta
4 cups water
Salt to taste
2 tablespoons olive oil
1 onion, diced
2 cloves garlic, minced
1 red bell pepper, diced
1 yellow bell pepper, diced
1 zucchini, diced
1 eggplant, diced
1 can (14.5 oz) diced tomatoes
1 teaspoon dried basil
1 teaspoon dried thyme
Freshly ground black pepper to taste
1/4 cup Parmesan cheese, grated (optional)
Fresh basil leaves for garnish

SERVES 4

COOK THE POLENTA: Bring water to a boil in a large saucepan. Slowly whisk in the polenta and salt. Reduce heat to low and cook, stirring frequently, until thickened, about 5-7 minutes. Cover and keep warm.

SAUTÉ THE AROMATICS: While the polenta is cooking, heat the olive oil in a large skillet over medium heat. Add the onion and garlic and cook until the onion is translucent, about 3-4 minutes.

ADD THE VEGETABLES: Add the bell peppers, zucchini, and eggplant to the skillet. Cook, stirring occasionally, until the vegetables are tender, about 5-7 minutes.

ADD THE TOMATOES AND HERBS: Stir in the diced tomatoes, dried basil, and dried thyme. Season with salt and freshly ground black pepper. Cover and simmer for 10 minutes to let the flavors meld.

SERVE: Serve the ratatouille over the warm polenta. Sprinkle with Parmesan cheese, if desired, and garnish with fresh basil leaves.

RISOTTO PRIMAVERA

INGREDIENTS:

1 tablespoon olive oil
1 small onion, finely chopped
2 cloves garlic, minced
1 cup Arborio rice
1/2 cup dry white wine
4 cups low-sodium vegetable broth, heated
2 cups mixed spring vegetables (such as asparagus, peas, and bell peppers), chopped
1/2 cup Parmesan cheese, grated
Salt and pepper to taste
Chopped fresh basil or parsley, for garnish

SERVES 4

SAUTÉ THE AROMATICS: Heat the olive oil in a large skillet over medium heat. Add the onion and garlic, and sauté until the onion is translucent, about 5 minutes.

TOAST THE RICE: Add the Arborio rice to the skillet, stirring to coat in the oil. Cook until the rice is lightly toasted, about 2 minutes.

DEGLAZE THE PAN: Pour in the wine, stirring constantly, until it has been absorbed by the rice.

COOK THE RISOTTO: Begin adding the hot vegetable broth to the rice, one ladle at a time, stirring continuously. Wait until each ladle of broth has been absorbed before adding the next. This process should take about 10-12 minutes.

ADD THE VEGETABLES: When you have one ladle of broth left, add the spring vegetables to the skillet. Continue to cook, adding the last of the broth, until the vegetables are tender and the rice is creamy.

FINISH THE RISOTTO: Stir in the Parmesan cheese, and season with salt and pepper to taste. Remove from heat.

SERVE: Divide the risotto between four plates. Garnish with fresh basil or parsley, and serve hot.

SOBA NOODLES WITH GINGER SESAME DRESSING

COOK THE NOODLES: Cook the soba noodles according to package instructions, then rinse under cold water to cool and stop the cooking process.

PREPARE THE DRESSING: While the noodles are cooking, combine all dressing ingredients in a jar and shake well to combine. You can also whisk them together in a bowl.

COMBINE THE INGREDIENTS: In a large bowl, combine the cooked soba noodles, red bell pepper, cucumber, and green onions.

DRESS THE NOODLES: Drizzle the ginger sesame dressing over the noodle mixture. Toss until everything is well coated.

SERVE: Sprinkle with sesame seeds before serving.

INGREDIENTS:

8 ounces of soba noodles
1 red bell pepper, thinly sliced
1 english cucumber, thinly sliced
2 green onions, sliced thinly
2 tablespoons of sesame seeds

FOR THE GINGER SESAME DRESSING:
2 tablespoons of sesame oil
2 tablespoons of soy sauce
1 tablespoon of rice vinegar
1 tablespoon of fresh ginger, grated
1 clove garlic, minced
1 tablespoon of honey
1 teaspoon of sriracha (optional)

SERVES 4

SPINACH AND FETA FRITTATA

INGREDIENTS:

8 large eggs
Salt and pepper to taste
2 tablespoons olive oil
1 small onion, finely chopped
2 cloves garlic, minced
4 cups fresh spinach
1/2 cup feta cheese, crumbled
1 tablespoon fresh dill, chopped

SERVES 4

PREPARE THE EGGS: In a large bowl, beat the eggs until well combined. Season with salt and pepper to taste.

SAUTÉ THE AROMATICS: Heat the olive oil in a large, oven-safe skillet over medium heat. Add the chopped onion and cook until it becomes translucent, about 3-5 minutes. Add the minced garlic and cook until fragrant, about 1 minute.

ADD THE SPINACH: Add the spinach to the skillet. Cook, stirring occasionally, until the spinach has wilted, about 2-3 minutes.

ADD THE EGGS: Pour the beaten eggs over the spinach mixture in the skillet. Cook without stirring until the edges start to set, about 2 minutes.

ADD THE FETA AND DILL: Sprinkle the crumbled feta cheese and chopped dill evenly over the top of the eggs.

BAKE THE FRITTATA: Preheat the broiler of your oven. Place the skillet under the broiler and cook until the frittata is set and golden brown on top, about 3-4 minutes. Watch closely to prevent overcooking.

SERVE: Remove the skillet from the oven (remember the handle will be hot!) and let the frittata cool for a few minutes. Cut into slices and serve warm.

SWEET POTATO AND BLACK BEAN TACOS

COOK THE POTATOES: In a large skillet, heat the olive oil over medium heat. Add the sweet potatoes and season with cumin, chili powder, salt, and pepper. Cook until the sweet potatoes are tender, about 7-10 minutes.

ADD THE BEANS: Add the black beans and salsa to the skillet, stirring well to combine. Cook for an additional 2-3 minutes until everything is heated through.

PREPARE THE TORTILLAS: Warm the tortillas in a dry skillet over medium heat, turning once.

ASSEMBLE THE TACOS: To assemble the tacos, place a scoop of the sweet potato and black bean mixture on each tortilla. Top with slices of avocado and a sprinkle of fresh cilantro.

SERVE: Serve the tacos with lime wedges on the side for squeezing.

INGREDIENTS:

2 large sweet potatoes, peeled and diced
1 tablespoon of olive oil
1 teaspoon of ground cumin
1 teaspoon of chili powder
1 can (15 oz) of black beans, drained and rinsed
1/2 cup of salsa
8 small whole wheat tortillas
1 avocado, sliced
1/2 cup of fresh cilantro, chopped
Salt and black pepper to taste
Lime wedges for serving

SERVES 4